TIGER TERRITORY

A Story of the Chitwan Valley

by Ann Whitehead Nagda

Illustrated by Paul Kratter

Soundprints
Where Children Discover...

For my husband, Jagdish — A.W.N.

*To my loving family, Joel, Marshall, and Tia. This book is also
dedicated to preserving the natural habitat of the magnificent tiger* — P.K.

Illustrations copyright © 1999 Paul Kratter
Book copyright © 1999 Trudy Corporation, 353 Main Avenue, Norwalk, CT 06851.

Soundprints is a division of Trudy Corporation, Norwalk, Connecticut.

Book layout: Diane Hinze Kanzler
Editor: Judy Gitenstein

First Edition 1999
10 9 8 7 6 5 4 3 2 1
Printed in Hong Kong

Acknowledgments:
  Our thanks to Fiona Sunquist, Bengal tiger specialist, for her curatorial review.

  The author would like to thank Bhim Gerung and Dave Smith for their invaluable help
in researching tigers at Chitwan National Park.

Library of Congress Cataloging-in-Publication Data

Nagda, Ann Whitehead
    Tiger territory: a story of the Chitwan Valley / written by Ann Whitehead Nagda;
illustrated by Paul Kratter.
        p.   cm.
    Summary: A tigress roams the Chitwan Valley in southern Nepal in search of food for
herself and her three cubs.
    ISBN 1-56899-720-5 (hardcover)   ISBN 1-56899-721-3 (pbk.)
    1. Tigers — Juvenile fiction. [1. Tigers — Fiction.] I. Kratter, Paul, ill.   II. Title.
PZ10.3.N14Ti   1999
[Fic] — dc21
                                                                            98-42571
                                                                            CIP
                                                                            AC

TIGER TERRITORY

A Story of the Chitwan Valley

by Ann Whitehead Nagda

Illustrated by Paul Kratter

The
Nature
Conservancy®

Thick winter fog blankets the Chitwan Valley in southern Nepal. It muffles the calls of migrating bar-headed geese as they fly over the swampy lowlands. Coarse blades of grass, some rising twenty feet high, drip with moisture. Hidden in the tall grass, a Bengal tigress watches a herd of chital deer grazing by the river.

A kingfisher dives into the water, then flies up with a fish in its bill. The tigress steals closer to the deer. She tenses, ready to spring. Suddenly, one of the chitals sniffs the air, catches the scent of tiger and cries out a shrill warning. With tails raised, the herd scatters.

The tigress stands up and stretches. She will have to hunt something else, but now she enters the forest along a narrow path. She follows a stream bed to a ravine thick with shrubs and softly calls "ahh-oooo, ahh-oooo." One male and two female tiger cubs rush from a bamboo thicket. They greet their mother with excited squeaks as they run around her in circles. They are very hungry.

The tigress nuzzles her cubs, then sprawls on her side to let them nurse. They are six months old and their teeth are sharp. After a few minutes their mother stands and shakes them off. Flicking her tail, she walks a few paces away and sits down. The three cubs climb on her again, eager for more milk.

To keep her growing cubs satisfied, the mother tigress must make a kill every few days. She leads the cubs through a forest of sal trees and scattered phoenix palms. A sloth bear sucks termites from a castle-shaped mound. The tigress edges her cubs away from the fierce and unpredictable bear.

The male cub clambers up a fig tree. Above him, langur monkeys cackle with alarm and leap away. This disturbs some green parakeets, who swoop through the treetops, squawking loudly. One of the female cubs starts to follow her brother into the tree, but he defends his territory and playfully pushes her down.

Emerging from the forest, the tigress and her cubs approach an oxbow lake. The lake was created when the nearby river changed course, leaving a loop of water in the shape of a large bow. The morning fog has burned off and the distant white peaks of the Himalayan mountains glow in the sunlight. A huge, one-horned rhino stands in the water. Two mynah birds land on the rhino's back and begin to search its thick hide for ticks. Near the banks, several young wild pigs root in the swampy earth. The tigress crouches and moves toward them.

There is little sound beside the rustling of the dry grasses and the contented grunts of the piglets. Storks probe the mud along the shoreline for snails. The tigress creeps closer. Suddenly, a peacock flies up out of the tall grass, chased by the three tiger cubs. Several peafowl scream and the piglets let out a chorus of squeals.

Grunting furiously, a huge wild sow charges out of the tall grass to stand guard in front of her piglets. She snorts, ready to do battle with her sharp tusks. The tigress decides not to tangle with the ferocious mother pig and calls the cubs to follow her.

The cubs scamper after their mother. She leads them now toward the river. Near the bank is a grove of silk cotton trees, ablaze with large red flowers. Rhesus macaques sit on the tree branches. They stick their faces into the flowers to drink the sweet nectar. Pollen clings to their furry faces. As the monkeys move from blossom to blossom through the trees, they pollinate the flowers. Some of the flowers fall to the ground, where chital deer crowd beneath the tree, eating them eagerly. When she sees this, the tigress crouches low into the grass.

The cubs watch as their mother stalks the herd. Unaware, a chital moves toward her as it sniffs for flowers. The tigress charges from her hiding place and bites through the nape of the chital's neck with her teeth. Lapwings fly into the air and screech a warning. The other deer flee.

The tigress carries the dead chital into the tall grass and calls to her cubs. Just as they begin to eat, a young male tiger approaches, snarling. This is not the father of the cubs, but a strange tiger passing through their territory. The tigress knows that he might hurt her cubs. She grunts a warning and quickly leads them away. To save her babies, she must let the stranger have the chital.

The mother tigress takes her cubs to safety near their den in the bamboo thicket. She backs into the nearby stream, takes a drink, then sits in the water to cool herself. She swishes her tail up, showering her back with water. When she comes out of the water she lies under a tree and watches as the male cub stalks another peacock. The two female cubs lie down by their mother and whine because they are hungry. The tigress licks them with her raspy tongue.

Later, back in the den, the cubs fall asleep in a furry heap. Their mother leaves them to return to her hunting.

The tigress heads back to the spot where she killed the chital deer. Before she gets there she can hear tigers fighting. As she comes near, she sees that one is her mate—the father of her cubs—and the other is the young male who stole her kill. With a roar, her mate rises on his hind legs and slaps at the intruder. Vultures squabble behind them over all that is left of the deer carcass.

The tigress slips away. All night long she hunts alone. With a fluid grace, she strides along forest paths and follows stream beds. She waits patiently beside water holes, but does not catch anything.

In the early morning the tigress returns to her cubs. They rub against her body in greeting and playfully grab at her tail.

The tigress leads the cubs through the forest. The cubs chase and tumble over each other, racing far ahead. All at once, a sambar calls out in alarm.

Startled by her rowdy cubs, a frightened sambar stag bounds toward the tigress. The tigress leaps up and grasps the sambar by its throat. The sambar shakes her off. The tigress grabs its hind leg and brings the stag to the ground, but it scrambles up and runs away.

The tigress races after the injured stag and overtakes it near the oxbow lake. She clamps her teeth on its throat and the stag falls at the edge of the water. A marsh mugger crocodile slides into the water and swims toward the sambar. Snarling, the tigress slaps the water with her paw to keep the crocodile away. Then she drags the carcass away from the water's edge while the cubs leap about in excitement. As they settle down to feast, a large male tiger comes toward them out of the forest.

This time it is the cubs' father. He sits nearby, waiting to eat until the mother and cubs have had their fill. A tree-pie lands on the carcass, but the tigress swats it with her paw. Vultures gather in a tree nearby, waiting their turn.

When the tigers have finished eating, the mother tigress licks one of the female cubs. The other female cub goes to nuzzle her father, then returns to stretch out and lazily bat at her sister's tail. The male cub lies down by his mother's head. With full stomachs they all rest near the remains of their meal, their hunger satisfied at last.

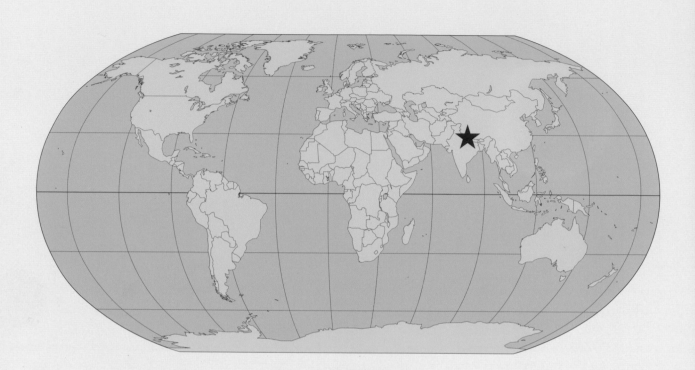

Chitwan National Park, Nepal

Chitwan National Park was established in 1973 to protect an area where Bengal tigers live. The main needs of a Bengal tiger are water, plentiful prey, and ample cover for den areas and for hiding while stalking prey. At Chitwan, tigers find all of these in abundance.

About Chitwan National Park

The fertile grasslands and swamps of Chitwan are nourished by rivers which overflow their banks during the monsoon rains, spreading rich silt on either side. After the rains, twenty-foot-high grasses grow from these deposits. During days of intense summer heat, many animals seek shelter in the sal forests which cover Chitwan's hillsides.

Bengal tigers can thrive in many different habitats, from dry, thorn forests to mangrove swamps, where they will swim between islands. Male tigers mark out a territory with their scent to warn other adult males away, and will fight any strange male brazen enough to ignore the warning. The male patrols his marked territory, which includes the smaller territories of several female mates and their cubs. A mother tigress provides food for her cubs for nearly two years while she teaches them to hunt and fend for themselves.

At one time, few people lived in this lowland area of southern Nepal because mosquitoes from the swamps spread malaria. Now, since scientific and medical progress has solved much of that problem, farms and villages surround the park. This has created new problems: Rhinos, monkeys, and deer wander out of the park to feast in the farmers' fields. Tigers stalk and kill livestock. To make it up to the local farmers, the park allows them inside each year to harvest some of the tall grass. The farmers use the grass for building the walls and roofs of their houses and for making rope, fences, baskets, fish traps, and scarecrows.

Recently, the local people have also become involved in reforestation projects. They replanted trees, built a mud dam, cleared land for a grassland habitat, and constructed a wildlife viewing tower. The local people receive half the money earned from tourism, which they use to improve and support their schools and health clinic. This conservation project is a model of what can be done to involve people in saving the local habitat of endangered species.

In spite of these good efforts, tigers are still hunted illegally by poachers for use in traditional Chinese medicines. People believe medicines made from tiger bone and other tiger parts can cure many ailments, and they will pay highly for them. Because of this, as well as the loss of wild habitat, it is estimated that only 3,000–5,000 Bengal tigers remain in the wild.

Organizations around the world are trying to help. Exxon Corporation has started a worldwide "Save the Tiger" campaign with the U.S. National Fish and Wildlife Foundation. The World Wildlife Fund, the National Geographic Society, and the Wildlife Conservation Society support tiger conservation. These organizations are working together to launch a plan to save tigers, focusing on some common goals: the protection of critical tiger habitats; the closing down of North American markets for tiger products; ending the demand for medicines using tiger parts with a public-awareness campaign, *Destroy the Myth, Not the Tiger*; and a renewed effort to raise funds for tiger conservation.

Glossary

▲ *Bar-headed geese*

▲ *Lapwing*

▲ *Peacock*

▲ *Common kingfisher*

▲ *Marsh mugger crocodile*

▲ *Rhesus macaque*

▲ *Greater one-horned rhinoceros*

▲ *Mynah bird*

▲ *Sambar*

▲ *Green parakeet*

▲ *Wild boar sow and piglets*

▲ *Bengal tiger*

▲ *Elephant grass*

▲ *Sloth bear*

▲ *Chital deer*

▲ *Langur monkey*

▲ *White-backed vultures*

▲ *Sal trees*